STUDENT ATHLETE 101

College Life Made Easy On & Off The Field

ANTONIO NEVES

ISBN: 1449978606
ISBN-13: 9781449978600
Library of Congress Control Number: 2010900345

CONTENTS

This book is dedicated to all collegiate student-athletes who believe that giving up simply isn't an option.

INTRODUCTION

As a high school teenager in Jackson, Michigan, I was an average student with an average 2.6 GPA. My grades were definitely nothing to brag about. But as a jock, I had some skills and was recruited by colleges for football and track and field. Eventually, I selected Western Michigan University (WMU) and decided to pursue track and field, instead of football. At WMU, I was a "preferred walk-on," which meant my scholarship wasn't just handed to me. I had to earn it, and I eventually did – all $2,000 a year of it.

During my first semester at WMU, I surprised myself by earning a 3.6 GPA. I must have done a few things right! Sports always came naturally for me, but academics required more effort. After the initial shock wore off, I was determined to figure out how I could do so well in an area where I was historically average. Before long, I realized the answer was right in front of me. I just needed to apply myself to my studies with the same passion I put into my athletics.

My success in that first semester and throughout my college years wasn't because of one particular action, but a variety. Yet, the one thing that stood out was that I began to care about how I performed in the classroom, similar to how I cared about my performance in track and field. Ultimately, excelling in academics became a personal challenge that I took very seriously. I realized how my time in college would affect the rest of my life. Plus, I began to see that my athletic career, like that of the vast majority of NCAA student-athletes, wouldn't last too long after graduation. Buzz kill.

But I had the confidence from my experience as a successful athlete on my side, and it didn't take long to transfer it to the classroom. The classroom became the field where I met my competitors – the assignments and the exams. I was determined to win at all costs. Just as I practiced on the track to qualify for a major competition, I used that same focus and discipline to excel in the classroom. I realized that in order to achieve success, I simply needed to believe in myself and put forth an honest effort. And that is exactly what I did. Using the 3 D's, taught to me by a high school coach – Desire, Discipline and Dedication – I knew I could achieve success not only on the track, but in the classroom and life.

Despite the demands of being a Division I student-athlete, occasionally working a part-time job, and staying involved on campus, I gradually found academic success. I discovered there is a strategy to attaining success in college and it can be applied by virtually every student. The same approach I used can lead to success for you too. I can't guarantee you'll get a 3.5 GPA just by reading this book (it requires your effort and motivation too). But I can guarantee that this book will show you how to take advantage of every opportunity available, so you can maximize the benefits of these life-changing college years now, and for years to come.

In some ways I stumbled upon my success in college. You may be stumbling too, but having a harder time reaching your goals. I wrote *Student Athlete 101* for you. I did a few things right and unlocked the secret to success in academics and athletics that will even extend to your professional life after college. These "right" things can help you as you transition from high school to university life. Even if you have some college experience under your belt but you're not encountering the success you want, this guide will be useful in turning things around. This guide is for all student-athletes, regardless of your sport, gender or academic background.

Student Athlete 101 is relevant and practical. It's not your typical college textbook. You'll find recommendations and strategies to make your college experience rewarding from the very first day you set foot on campus. You won't find confusing theories, clichéd techniques or ineffective short cuts. The guide is straightforward and created with you in mind. That said, there might be sections that are more valuable to you than others. Focus on those sections, put them into action and make this guide work for you.

In a nutshell, *Student Athlete 101* is an invaluable resource that will support you throughout your college experience. Being a student-athlete is a privilege. Don't take it for granted. I want you to get the most out of your entire college experience, from the classroom to the gym and well after you graduate. You only live once, so knock it out of the park. Make this once-in-a-life opportunity a catalyst for your future successes. GOOD LUCK!

Antonio Neves
Western Michigan University, Class of 1999
All Mid American Conference, Triple Jumper & Academic Team
Columbia University Graduate School of Journalism, Class of 2006

Chapter 1
WHAT TO EXPECT

The day you've been waiting for has finally arrived! When you first set foot on campus, you'll probably scream at the top of your lungs, "I'm free!" And actually, this is relatively true. With the exception of your coaches and your academic advisors, you are responsible for the choices you make in college. The buck stops with you. College introduces a lot of responsibility that you've probably never experienced before. Are you ready?

Adjustment

With your arrival to campus, "college life" has just begun. You've just moved into your dorm room, probably with someone you've never met before; you're still trying to figure out what you ate for lunch in the café; and there are tons of people approaching you (or maybe not) who want to be your friend. Various student organizations, fraternities, and sororities are doing their best to snag your attention. You overhear there's a party tonight, tomorrow, and just about every day until the end of the semester. The first football game is Saturday (maybe you're in it!) and there is something you're trying to remember…oh! Classes begin tomorrow, and you have practice. Great way to start things out, huh? This is an extreme, but realistic, example of what you'll experience in the first few days and weeks of school. So lace up your sneakers and be prepared.

Here's your first tip: Before you get too excited or over-whelmed, take a moment to just sit back, enjoy, and take it all in. Do your best not to over analyze the situation, or most importantly, react in a naïve way. Enjoy the euphoria of these first few days for what it is - college life at its best. Plus, situations like these won't just occur during the first couple weeks of school, but throughout your college career. You'll have external forces pulling you in every direction. Here's one example that comes about quite often: "Should I study tonight or go to that party?" There will be many tough decisions to be made (at least they feel tough), but take a deep breath and relax.

Right now is the perfect opportunity for you to evaluate your priorities and choose the ones that are most important to you. Ideally they should be in this order: academics, athletics, and social life. Depending upon your sport, you may be taught that athletics are your first priority. Don't get it twisted. You're on campus to get an education.

It's important to understand that the microscope is <u>always</u> on student-athletes, which makes all the choices you make important too. Always use your best judgment by evaluating the immediate and long-term effect of them. At the same time, you don't need to over-analyze every situation. Sometimes you should just go with your gut instinct. There is nothing wrong with being spontaneous and unpredictable from time to time, as long as you're aware of the consequences. Remember, life without taking a few risks is a life not lived. Yet there is a major distinction between taking a risk and doing something flat out stupid. You will make many mistakes. Mistakes are okay because they add up to experience and ultimately build the character you need to succeed. This assumes, of course, that you don't end up in jail, kicked off your team or expelled from your university. Unfortunately, these things happen to some of the most promising student-athletes. You may want to make headlines, but not career-ending ones.

Where Do You Fit In?

The best environment for you is the one you feel most comfortable in. As an athlete, you'll be exposed to a unique environment that is the envy of your non-athlete peers. I confess there's something special (and fun) about being known as student-athlete on campus. Even still, there are times when you'd rather be an ordinary student because the life of a student-athlete isn't always as glamorous as it appears. That's why it's a good thing to build a community outside your student-athlete peers.

Over time you'll develop an inner circle of friends that includes your teammates or fellow jocks, but brings together a diverse collection of people from around the campus. Look beyond external attributes like "jock status," and seek out people who compliment you and your goals. It doesn't make sense to spend time with people who are counterproductive to your success in the classroom and within your sport. Spend time with people who are positive and optimistic. Be open to getting to know people who are different than you and your normal crowd. Yes, that means looping non-athletes into your inner circle.

During my collegiate career, I watched as student-athletes spent their entire college career enclosed in a tight circle of only athletes. Eventually they regretted this, and so will you. Successful people are open-minded and are diverse thinkers. This can only come from associating with people outside of your norm. Different doesn't mean better or worse. It just means different. Keep an open-mind and an optimistic outlook. Everything else will naturally fall into place.

HELPFUL HINTS

1. When making choices, evaluate the short and long-term effects of your choice. As a student-athlete, you'll be judged differently than the general student body.
2. Surround yourself with positive and optimistic people.
3. Develop relationships with people that are different than you. That means meeting people outside of the athletic realm.

Chapter 2
ORGANIZING & PRIORITIZING

Organization

Before college you may have lived an organized life, or maybe not. Either way, college adds new challenges that require you to brush up on some basic organization skills, even before you take your first quiz or exam. These skills allow you to be more effective and less stressed about fulfilling your new responsibilities as a student-athlete. That translates to better overall performance.

Organizational approaches vary greatly between students. Some organize their days to the minute, while some just go with the flow. The key is to create a system that works best for you and your natural style. But you must have a system! As a student-athlete, it is imperative to be extremely disciplined with your time, because it will be stretched to the limit with the demands of class work, team meetings, practices, travel time and more.

Your first step should be to purchase a daily planner. The best gift I ever received as a student was a day planner. It made all the difference in my academic, athletic, and personal life. Eventually I came to the point where I felt lost without it. Personally, I prefer paper planners, but in this age of technology, an electronic organizer may be a better choice for you. Choose what makes you feel the most comfortable, test drive it for a while, and then stick with it.

Your planner is the hub that keeps your college life on track. From the moment you receive a class syllabus and a schedule of your athletic obligations, transfer those important dates to your planner. That includes everything from when assignments are due, exam dates, practice times, and meetings to when you'll be traveling or going on vacation. Putting everything in a single place makes it easier to keep track of it all. Things tend to slip through the cracks when you keep them scattered in binders, individual syllabi, and stray fliers. Having a central organizing hub also helps if changes occur, like new assignments or practice cancellations. Your planner gives you a bird's eye view of your entire college life, so you know what fits and how. Use your planner to store all appointments and personal information, even those outside of your athletic or classroom responsibilities (i.e. doctor appointments, dates, etc.).

Time is a commodity when you're a student-athlete. Don't squander it! The extra effort you put into being organized will pay off. You'll know exactly when, where and what is happening in your busy life. You'll be prepared. You'll be relaxed. You'll impress your peers, coaches and professors. The biggest payoff - you'll excel in your academics and in your sport. And remember, you are solely responsible for your success. Staying organized enables that success. Make your planner your best friend and take care of it. Eventually you will get to the point where you cannot live without it.

Prioritizing

Every day, preferably first thing in the morning or the evening before, you should review your planner and figure out your day's action plan. Ask: *what do I want to accomplish today?* Also look ahead to see what upcoming projects are due or when you'll be on the road with your team. As you review your daily events and longer-term activities, decide what needs to be completed today and put those activities in order of importance. This is prioritizing, or ranking tasks in order of importance. For example, which task is more important, studying for tomorrow's exam or completing the term paper that is due in two months? Gradually you will develop a system for prioritizing. It's as simple as looking at your calendar.

I'm sure you've met people who don't have a clue about what's going on. They're always late and unprepared. Don't let that be you. Always stay on top of your responsibilities, all of them. As a student-athlete, more is expected of you. People are watching. Don't make this responsibility harder than it needs to be. Get organized now, even if you think it's not necessary. It's better to be safe than sorry. Besides, organization and prioritization skills will be a major benefit to you in college and far beyond these years. Don't let your responsibilities run you, run them!

HELPFUL HINTS

1. Purchase a daily planner – paper or electronic.
2. Transfer all academic, athletic, and personal tasks, activities and goals into your planner.
3. Always keep your planner current; update it frequently.
4. Prioritize your many responsibilities in order of importance and follow through with them.
5. Take control of your life!

Chapter 3
BUILDING RELATIONSHIPS WITH STUDENTS, COACHES & PROFESSORS

Students

It's widely known that you become most like those with whom you associate, so it's in your best interest to surround yourself with the right people early in your college career. Think about people you know, or know of, who are successful. What do they have in common? Chances are they're focused, driven, and positive – just to name a few attributes. Athletes or not, find these students and get to know them. Network! Networking is developing relationships that offer mutually beneficial rewards for each party, today and down the road. Your network is the foundation of your success, so don't wait to start building it. You can network in the locker room, the classroom, the cafeteria, the frat party; networking can happen just about anywhere. Plus, you may be surprised at the friendships you gain as you network toward your academic, professional, and personal success.

You already know that before heading into my first year of college, I was a mediocre student with atrocious study habits. Although I didn't like it at first, I was assigned to the honors dormitory instead of the usual "jock" dorms. The honors dorm was the last place I wanted to be, but it ended up being the best thing that could have ever happened to me. At first, it seemed that my "average intelligence" was a hindrance. I wondered how I'd fit in with my student-athlete mentality. However, I began noticing a change in my behavior. For example, I had an extremely smart room-mate, and when he studied, I would study. When he went to the library to research a topic or study, I would occasionally tag along. In the beginning, I tagged along in response to my competitive nature; I couldn't let this guy be better than me! But gradually his habits became my habits, and they were good ones to have. It didn't take long for me to integrate with the honors students. I began to develop relationships with my new peers and actually enjoyed spending time with them in the study lounge. I discovered that there was no major difference between these "gifted" students and myself from an academic standpoint, except for one thing - they *applied* themselves. And the best news? A few of the students I met in the honors dorm are some of my closest friends today.

The lesson I learned from that experience is this: when you're placed in a new environment, you'll adapt. In my case, I adapted to a situation that improved my life. I learned a great deal from the other students, and I'm sure I taught them a thing or two as well. Of course, it would have been easier for me to live in the jock dorm, but I took a risk and stuck it out in the honors dorm. It paid off and I don't regret it. I couldn't have had the same academic success if I were any place else.

By the way, I'm not suggesting that you have to live in the honors dorms to succeed in school. Rather you must surround yourself with people who are academically strong, wherever they live. Here's a good rule of thumb: if you're the smartest person in the room, or in your group of friends, something is wrong and it's time to expand your network. Let go of the "nerds versus jocks" stereotypes. Grow up and recognize the importance of having a wide and diverse network. You may find yourself in my situation where some of the students you used to call "nerds" become your closest friends. Or, one day your teammates might call you a "nerd," which is really a compliment.

Professors

The professor-student relationship can be intimidating for an entering freshman. You obviously look to your professors as authority figures who have control of your academic future. But don't underestimate your power in the relationship. The college landscape is much different than the high school landscape. It's perfectly acceptable to view your professors as your equals, so long as you understand that you each contribute something unique to the relationship. And remember, the sole purpose of a professor is to be there for you, the student. If you break it down, your tuition is paying their salary, so technically they work for you! When you think of it that way, you have the edge in the relationship, and it helps minimize the intimidation factor. But don't get cocky. You must still respect the relationship dynamic so you don't get on the wrong side of your professors. You're a student-athlete, and that makes you unique. But you're not special. You're just in a special situation. Nobody owes you anything. You have to earn it.

To start, make a commitment to develop a professional relationship with all of your professors. The best way to do this is by attending their office hours, even if you don't have a pressing problem to address. Plan to visit your professors two to three times a month. Initially, you might set aside time to introduce yourself so they know you beyond the name printed on their class roster. Show them the human behind the name by sharing a bit about yourself and why you're taking their class. Let them know you're a student-athlete and that your hectic schedule may cause you to miss class, but you're committed to doing well. The main point you want to emphasize is that you care about your grades and their class. You may find them to be empathetic to your situation and end up receiving some leniency during the class. But don't walk in expecting this! Be careful not to imply that you're looking for (or expect) a free handout or easy "A." It will backfire and damage your relationship.

Next, learn a little about your professor's teaching style and their expectations. Each professor has a unique approach that may be unlike what you've experienced before, so take time early in the class to understand your professor's preferences. Most professors appreciate proactive students. That means coming to your professor early if you have the slightest problem or confusion, rather than waiting until the very last second to address the situation. Your professor is managing many students, not just you. Give him or her the benefit of time, which actually enables him or her to better assist you when you're in need. Think about it, if a problem does arise (i.e. bad result on an exam, missed assignment, etc.) the professor already knows who you are, sees your willingness to learn, and may be more than willing to help you in return. You don't want to be the student who never asked for help, failed the first two exams, and then hours before the final exam begs the professor for help and leniency. It's not likely to happen.

Keep in mind, the size of your university and classes will determine the accessibility of your professors. Normally, it's mandatory for professors to conduct office hours and if they're not available, a Teachers Assistant (TA) is available for consultation. If you find it difficult to meet with the professor in person, don't let that stop you. With technology, professors and students have e-mail accounts, class message boards and voice mail at their disposal. Exhaust all available means of communication to stay connected with your professor, even if it means going through the athletic department or your academic advisors to do so.

I should pause here to remind you that I'm not asking you to stalk your professors. Just stay connected and give them the opportunity to get to know you beyond your student-athlete status. Unfortunately, student-athletes have a bad reputation in the classroom. Don't contribute to the negative stereotypes. Change the course. Set a good example so it's easier for the next student-athlete. It's one of the responsibilities of the role. And remember, professors see hundreds of students a day, which means it's easy to get lost in the crowd. Taking time to set yourself apart as an individual makes a big difference.

And one last important reminder – fostering a relationship with your professors is actually networking, and as I described before, networking can develop into meaningful friendships and important business connections down the road.

Coaches

It's said that coaches and athletes have a love-hate relationship. For the most part, I found this to be true.

However, you can enjoy more of the love side of that relationship with positive communication. That begins with understanding a coach's perspective. Generally he or she views the student-athlete as an investment, whether you're receiving a scholarship or not. Similar to the stock market, return on investment (ROI) matters. Each coach employs different tactics and strategies to maximize a student-athlete's ROI. Without sounding too harsh, you'll have to adjust if you want to stay on the team. While it's nice to think that all coaches have your individual interests in mind 100 percent of the time, it's just not always the case.

But you can still create a win-win relationship with your coach by using many of the same tactics I suggested you use with professors. Get to know your coaches. Let them know your athletic and academic goals. Then take time to gain a better understanding of what they expect from you in both areas. Most relationships break down because of unclear expectations. Get clear. Make sure you and your coach are on the same page. And always be thoughtful about your coach's priorities, especially the student-athlete ROI I mentioned earlier.

Keep your relationship with your coach open and consistent. Don't disappear when things are going bad, academically or athletically. Your coach is a resource that can help you succeed. In fact, it's in your coach's best interest for this to happen! With this in mind, your coach will be understanding and patient. At the same time, you must remember your coach's priority – the student-athlete ROI. College sports are a big business, especially if you're in football or basketball. Athletic departments need to see immediate results from student-athletes because that translates into exposure for their program. This pressure for results is pushed down to your coach, and then to you. Be ready.

My best recommendation is for you to put your best effort forward in everything you do. Most importantly, don't take anything personal. College is a place of learning, so expect to get a lot of constructive (and maybe some not-so-constructive) feedback from your coaches and professors. No matter how the feedback lands, accept it as part of the learning process. Otherwise, you might go crazy. It's important to keep a light attitude even in the most stressful situations. Despite all the added responsibilities, college is supposed to be fun and your experience as a student-athlete is one you should enjoy. Isn't that why you first picked up that basketball, softball, volleyball, or hockey stick in the first place?

If you ever feel something isn't right from an athletic standpoint, don't hesitate to address this with your coach. If this doesn't provide the results you were looking for, talk to upperclassmen on your team or someone on the student-athlete advisory board. And if there isn't a board, recommend that the athletic department create one. Lastly, if all means have been exhausted with no results, contact a key person in the athletic department to discuss your issue.

I had a rewarding experience with my collegiate coach, and so can you. Like any relationship, it takes work - patience, persistence, and understanding. I was able to maintain a good relationship with my coach because I was patient and empathetic to his needs and concerns. You can do the same with your relationship with your coach. Nothing is more rewarding to a coach than your academic and athletic success. Obviously you'll benefit as well. In the end of your athletic career, your coach may know you better than anyone else in your life.

HELPFUL HINTS

1. Networking is developing relationships that offer mutually beneficial rewards for each party, today and down the road.
2. Surround yourself with students with similar academic goals.
3. Develop positive relationships with your professors, and visit with them at least two to three times a month.
4. Make it a priority to maintain consistent communication with your coaching staff.

Chapter 4
SOCIALIZING

———

College life offers endless opportunities for socializing and partying. "These are the best years of your life," isn't just a cliché, it's the truth, so go out and have a blast. Plus, you have the added benefit of being a student-athlete, which improves the dynamics of your social life by a lot. Enjoy! Just keep in mind that socializing encompasses more than parties and nightlife. Socializing also includes participating in student organizations, doing community service and engaging in other activities, both on and off campus. You're probably thinking, "I'll never have time for that with my full schedule!" And that's exactly the reason I devoted Chapter Two to organization. Stay on top of your priorities so you won't miss out on the fun. Of course, this is true to a point. I'd be lying to you if I promised that you would never miss some activities due to conflicts with your schedule or your values (some social activities just aren't acceptable for student-athletes). There's not much you can do about this but accept it. Being a student-athlete comes with great responsibility, and at times, sacrifice. You'll be faced with conflicts that make doing the right thing hard. But the benefits of being a student-athlete far outweigh the sacrifices you'll make.

I've always believed that the busier you are, the more focused you are and this can help you manage your on-campus activity. Here's just a glimpse of my life in college:

I balanced five classes a semester, played in a Division I NCAA sport, participated in numerous student organizations and occasionally held a part-time job. That may sound familiar to you, or you've become overwhelmed just imagining my activity. I'm not recommending that you do everything I did. Everyone is motivated in different ways. For me, having all of these obligations helped me be better organized, disciplined and focused. The key is finding the balance that works best for you. That means being active but not spreading yourself so thin that you're ineffective and performing poorly. After a semester or two, you'll get a better feel for your limits. Notice them and respond accordingly, but never underestimate yourself or your ability to do more than you've done before.

Student Organizations

Every campus offers a variety of student organizations you can participate in. You could join the American Marketing Association, Ski Club, or the International Students Organization, just to name a few. The best part of student organizations is that if you don't see one that fits your interests, you can start your own, which is a great leadership opportunity that will benefit you during college and beyond. There are also other alternatives for socializing that include social or professional fraternities and sororities, student government and hall council. The point is that there are plenty of opportunities to be involved on campus. Just evaluate the positives and negatives of each and make the choice that best fits your needs, interests and goals.

Your involvement in student organizations is a no-brainer, and a required element of your overall success. In

Chapter Three, I told you about building relationships and networking. This is an extension of that discussion. Joining one or more student organizations has numerous networking benefits, including: meeting new friends, developing solid connections, building your resume, and even releasing stress. Further, your involvement gives your resume a competitive edge post-graduation as future employers like to see how you've demonstrated ethics and skills that can be used at work. Another excellent reward of staying socially active is that you will increase your awareness of yourself and others.

Community Involvement

Student-athletes are leaders on the playing field, in the classroom, on campus and in their communities. Contributing to causes beyond your required obligations is a good thing and something worth pursuing. You might volunteer with a local foundation, hospital, community center, shelter or charity. Or better yet, start or become part of a community service outreach program with your team or the athletic department. As a student-athlete, you're an important and respected member of your local community, so lend a helping hand. Your university has tons of information available on volunteering opportunities.

Volunteering offers similar rewards to networking, but gives you even more as you make valuable contributions where they're needed most. That's priceless. You can be a mentor and share your knowledge with a local child, help build a house with Habitat for Humanity, or donate your time to a homeless shelter. Just talking to someone for a short time can make a major difference. The fundamental point is to share your time with others in need. Make a positive contribution to your community. More often than not, you'll get more out of the experience than you give.

<u>Getting Your Party On</u>

You didn't think I'd forget about fun social events did you? These would include parties, road trips, dating, sporting events, etc. It would be a huge waste of your college experience if you didn't participate in these activities. Go out and have fun! I'll let you in on a secret I discovered: the majority of learning actually takes place outside of the classroom, and I'm talking about academic smarts and life smarts. Besides, everyone deserves a break from the everyday stress of university life. You just need to know when to say when. Don't forget that as a student-athlete, you're judged differently than everyone else. People are watching, so make wise choices.

You, and only you, are responsible for your actions. Have fun, but don't be foolish. It doesn't make much sense to party until 4:00 am when you have an exam at 8:00 am. Further, there are certain parties or situations that, as a student-athlete, you just shouldn't be in. Be smart and think about the consequences of your actions before you leap in. You might need to miss "the party of the year," or put off meeting up with your friends, while you tend to other responsibilities. But if you think first and stay organized, you'll not only be on top of your responsibilities, but you'll make choices that enable your success. You can have your cake and eat it too. The key is distinguishing right from wrong and balancing your responsibilities effectively.

Remember, college is supposed to be the best years of your life. You don't want to spend every waking moment studying, but you also don't want to spend the rest of your life wishing you had worked a bit harder. College is supposed to be exciting, so have fun - SMART FUN.

HELPFUL HINTS

1. Join one or more student organizations.
2. Be active on campus and volunteer in your community.
3. Play it safe. Know when to say when and where you shouldn't be.
4. Have SMART FUN.

Chapter 5
EFFECTIVE STUDYING

Educators and students vary in their opinions about studying and how to do it right. I personally find the "keep it simple" approach works best, but you also need to do what works for you. Beyond this, remember that time isn't on your side. You have a lot of commitments, and procrastination is your worst enemy. Don't dig holes for yourself. Be prepared.

How to Take Notes

There are many ways to make studying easier and less time-consuming. Start by taking good in-class notes, and then make time to review your notes again later that day. Write down any questions or thoughts that pop into your head. Make a point to find the answers you need, whether you do it through independent research or meeting with your professor. You want to keep the material fresh in your mind so you don't forget it. A similar approach can be used when you're taking notes for reading assignments - take detailed notes while you're reading. Note any questions or ideas that come to mind as you read. Be thorough in your note taking, so that you won't waste time revisiting resources several times later.

Preparing for Exams

When you're studying, you should always have your exams or final papers in mind. But crunch time usually happens at least a week or more in advance. If you've prepared good study notes and have a good understanding of the content, preparation usually involves a simple review of your notes. But what if you're tackling a subject that challenges you? Then you'll need more time familiarizing yourself with the material. Familiarization comes from repetition and practice, the same two skills you use in your sport. Spend time between classes attending study groups or reviewing notes and practice exercises. Find a tutor. Meet with your professor. Do whatever helps you feel comfortable with the material. Like in your sport, you'll perform better on "game day" (also known as "exam day") when you're stress-free, prepared and confident in your abilities. It takes time to build that level of confidence in some subject areas, so don't procrastinate and wait until the last minute to prepare. Schedule intense study sessions, between 45 minutes to an hour, in the days preceding an exam to keep the material fresh in your mind. If you've started your preparation early and made your study sessions intense, you will not have to pull an all-nighter the day before the exam. Prepare in advance. Get your questions answered early. Be ready to tackle your exams with the same confidence you bring to your sport.

It's More Than Memorization

Inexperienced college students focus on memorizing material for exams. The problem with this approach is that it relies on your short-term memory, which is only capable of holding about four to nine bits of information at a time. To do well on exams, you have to figure out how to get more information into those four to nine bits. The best way to approach this is to simplify difficult or complex material into logical groups. Rather than memorize a multitude of small details, review your study notes, recall examples and illustrations from your professor and textbook, and then synthesize those details into four to nine groups, or "chunks," of information. For example, if you need to memorize the Periodic Table of Elements for a Chemistry class, you can chunk the elements into groups like alkali metals, metalloids, halogens, etc. Granted, this approach may not work with all subjects (i.e. calculus), but it does offer a new way to integrate foreign material into your mind for exams.

Pre-Test Your Knowledge Before the Big Day

When you've reached a point where you feel confident with the material, it's time to test yourself. Make and follow a checklist of what you need to know for the exam. Then, one by one, go down the list to decide if there are any areas where you might need to study more. When you're ready, you can perform a self-test using flash cards – testing your ability to recall information. You could also practice problems or spend time free writing about the material that will be on the exam. If your professor or teachers assistant (TA) is holding a review session, go! They do this for a reason and usually offer inside tips that will help you do well. Study groups can also be useful as you bounce ideas and questions around with other students. Any of these pre-test approaches will help your short-term memory recall of information. The added benefit is that you could learn something new that you need for the exam, or you could actually help others in the process.

Study Hard - Have Fun - Be Confident

Don't get so caught up in studying that you forget to have fun. You have a life that extends beyond the college campus. If you think your mind is on information overload, it probably is - relax a little. Step away from your studying to refresh yourself - workout, play video games, spend time with friends or just chill out for a bit.

Have I covered every study technique available? Not by any means. There are hundreds of ways to study. Some techniques will work for you, some won't. The tips I've offered here are the most common and tend to offer the most benefits. But as I've mentioned a few times before, you have to figure out what works for you. Develop a system that will allow you to get the most out of your studying without over-extending yourself. It may take a bit of trial and error, but you'll figure it out during your first few semesters. Most importantly – be confident. You're a college athlete for a reason. Bring the same confidence and drive used in your sport to the classroom. There are no handouts in life. Results and rewards come from investing your time wisely. That means being consistent in your actions, being positive in your attitude and focusing on solutions over problems.

Preparation pays off. While you may not receive A's on all your exams, you do earn respect. Besides, B's and C's build character (at least that's what you should tell your parents).

HELPFUL HINTS

1. Begin preparing for exams early.
2. Don't study - Review.
3. Test yourself and participate in review sessions or study groups.
4. Avoid memorizing details - Chunk it down instead.
5. Bring the same confidence you use in your sport to the classroom.

Chapter 6
USING FREE RESOURCES

———

Every university offers what I call "free resources." When you see free, take it! Examples of free resources include tutoring, counseling, advising and much more. As a student, you're entitled to these resources, but few students take full advantage of them. If you need academic assistance, you can get it – for free! From mathematics and sciences to English and foreign languages, you can get free help so you can be a better student. In the event you need help in a highly specialized area, like biomedical engineering, most related academic departments (in this example biology, chemistry or engineering) will offer some type of assistance, or at the very least, point you in the right direction. If you're not sure where to find help, visit your university's Academic Skills Center, or similarly named department, as a first step.

Did you know that as a student-athlete you're usually required to participate in *study-table* during your first few semesters. At a study-table, tutors typically are available and they're just for you. Don't pass on the opportunity to use this free resource! It's an advantage other students on campus don't have available.

<u>Help Outside Of The Classroom</u>

Your college likely offers help beyond academic support too. If you're going through a tough time in your life or feel like you need some emotional support, counseling is normally available through your university's health center – for free. Counselors on campus are trained in mental health and understand the issues relevant to students. Like physicians, your sessions with counselors are confidential. Don't be ashamed about using this free resource. College life isn't perfect. You will experience many ups and downs and talking to someone can help relieve the pressure you feel and help move you in the right direction. And sometimes talking to someone outside of your normal network of friends, family, coaches, and professors can help you gain the perspective you need. By the way, when you're not in college, meeting with a counselor can cost $75 per hour or more, so this is definitely a free resource worth using if you need it.

Don't ever be too proud to ask for help. You should already know this from your involvement in sports. Everyone needs a little help every once in a while. Even if you're not in dire need of help, it doesn't hurt to get a second opinion or to receive input from someone else. Who knows? You may learn something new. Campus resources and departments are designed for you and you'll get the most out of your collegiate career when you use them.

HELPFUL HINTS

1. Use every free resource when you need it.
2. Always stay open to receiving a second opinion or outside feedback.
3. During stressful and challenging times, talk to someone. Don't hide or hold in your troubles.

Chapter 7
SELECTING A MAJOR

———

Declaring your major is often one of the bigger pressures you'll have in college. Some will say that it's the single biggest decision of your life. While there is some truth in that point of view, it's also a bit over-dramatic. Did you know that a large number of college graduates don't even work directly in the field they studied? Choosing a major does not necessarily lock you into something you must do for the rest of your life. So breathe a little. Choosing your major is an important decision, but it's not a death sentence. Your major is simply a foundation, or launch pad, for where you might end up. One of the most beautiful things about life is how easily it can change or be different from what you ever imagined. There are theater majors that work in sales for top companies, biology majors who make careers in social work, and lawyers who do graphic design – the possibilities are endless. I'm a perfect example. I'm a marketing major who works in television and authored a book on a topic not related to broadcasting or marketing - go figure. The point is this, your major is important, in so far that you should pursue something you enjoy, but you always have the power to redirect your ultimate career path.

If you're going to devote four years of studying to something, why not choose something you're passionate about? Find an area that gets you excited! Unfortunately, you can't major directly in football, gymnastics, ice hockey or your sport, so look to other passions. Besides your sport, what is the one thing that you could do for the rest of your life, for free? You may not know right off the bat. Sometimes you have to test the waters before making a final decision. Students who change their major several times during their college career aren't necessarily indecisive. Exploring your options is smart, so long as you don't do it forever. Take time to reflect on your interests and natural ability. What gives you energy? What do you love to talk about? What have you always been curious about but never pursued? Dig deep, be open and you'll find the major that's best for you.

One of the challenges you'll face when choosing your major is pressure from the outside. Your parents may say, "I'm paying for this education, you'll study what I say." Or your coach might suggest, "Go for an 'easy' major so you can have time on the practice field." Listen to this feedback, but don't let outside pressures force you to pursue a major you have no interest in. In the end, you'll have to live with your major, not them. They won't be taking your exams and working hard for this degree, you will. Your education and area of study is your responsibility and yours alone. So select the major that's right for you.

If you're still a bit stuck and can't decide on a major, don't panic. Some students have known what they wanted to do for years, while others (like me) didn't figure it out until later. If you're in this boat, contact your university's Career Services office for help. The Career Services office provides information about a wide range of fields. You could get lost looking at all of them! But connect with someone in the Career Services office, and ask them to steer you in the right direction. Besides researching career fields, you might have access to career placement tests that can help nail down your interests and possible career paths. Remember though it's just information, and all career assessments are subjective. My test results said I'd be a good fashion model, which I thought was crazy at the time. But I did end up in a career in front of the television camera, so there might've been something to it.

One other very effective way to pick a major is to interview people in fields and industries where you might have an interest. Start with professors who teach in subject areas that interest you. Then try reaching out to local professionals or surf the Web to explore potential, post-graduate employers. Conducting these *informational interviews* will not only help you further define your choice of major, but it's also a great, non-intimidating way to practice interview skills you'll need when you graduate. At this point, you're not trying to get a job, so you'll be more comfortable contacting the human resources department of companies to inquire about careers. Be proactive. Don't be afraid to ask questions that uncover the realities of a profession either. Answers won't come to you; you must go to them. Get the information you need to make the best possible decision in your major.

Finally, don't make choosing a major a hyper-stressful experience. Most universities allow two years to declare your major, so enjoy being undeclared and really explore your options. Enjoy the general education (GE) courses you're required to take in your first two years and use the time to truly discover your passion. Maybe you're taking Astronomy to fulfill your physical science GE requirement, and discover that you love it. Explore the field, and if it's the right choice, select it as your major. If your passion decreases down the line, you can always change your major or redirect your career after college. Never limit yourself or your aspirations. Do what fulfills you, and never look back. That way you'll have no regrets in the end.

HELPFUL HINTS

1. Use your university's Career Service office, the Web and your network to research various careers and professions before picking a major.
2. Conduct informational interviews with professors and professionals in various fields.
3. Choose a career that you're passionate about and follow your dreams.

Chapter 8
EXPANDING YOUR HORIZONS: INTERNSHIPS & STUDYING ABROAD

———

If you haven't already noticed the underlying theme of this book, let me be clear - *college is a once in a lifetime experience and you should take advantage of everything it offers*. You can do this by trying something out of your norm. For example, you might attend a poetry reading, a cultural festival or a lecture on an unheard of topic. College is an excellent opportunity to do something out of the ordinary. Two incredible, out of the ordinary options for expanding your horizons are internships and studying abroad.

Wait! I already know what you're thinking, "I'm a student-athlete. I can't possibly commit to an internship or overseas study." You're right. Neither of these horizon-expanding opportunities will be easy to pursue, but neither is totally impossible either. So before you skip past this chapter, read on and just be open to the possibility.

Internships

You may be a star student-athlete with visions of a professional career in your sport. That's a vision to aspire to, so go for it! At the same time, remember that college, and everything it entails, prepares you for success in and out of your sport. Even if you are of the extremely small percentage of athletes who make it to the professional level, your professional career won't last forever. What will you do afterwards? If you want to be a step ahead of the competition, it's in your best interest to obtain an internship.

An internship is work experience in the field you'll enter after graduation. Some internships are paid, others are not. Both offer valuable experience that can build your resume, and your professional network. Plus, internships help solidify whether the area you've chosen is really a fit. You might also be surprised by where your internships take you. Maybe you'll land in Orlando with Walt Disney World, like I did, in Washington with Microsoft, with NBC in New York City or even overseas. The opportunities are endless but like most everything in college, you've got to go for what you want.

The best way to find an internship is to visit your university's Career Services office. They will usually post opportunities on a job board. They can also help you prepare for landing the internship by offering workshops about resume writing, interviewing techniques and professional behavior. Beyond the Career Services office, also plan to visit the academic department for your major. Sometimes the department has the inside scoop on internships in your field of study.

Outside of the Career Services office and your academic department, jobs fairs and the Internet are good resources for finding internships. Job fairs are an excellent opportunity for instant exposure to a variety of businesses in different industries. At the fair, you can speak to recruiters one-on-one and pass out your resume to prospective employers. Always arrive at job fairs ready to interview. That means being polished and dressed in professional attire. The Internet will also help in your search. Surf the Web to find companies that interest you and research possible internship opportunities.

As a student-athlete, you already have an big advantage over other students competing for internships, because you've already demonstrated qualities employers like to see - commitment to teamwork, ability to prioritize and multi-tasking and a strong work ethic. Use these attributes to your advantage during interviews. They will make you stand above and beyond the competition and leave no doubt who the best candidate is for the position.

Studying Abroad

Imagine studying in the rainforests of Costa Rica or discovering 16th century art in Italy. Now picture yourself on the beaches of Australia, participating in a Marine Biology class project. These opportunities should sound extremely exciting to any college student. Every now and then, students need a change of pace and studying abroad for a semester, summer or year could be just what you need.

A study abroad experience will give you a better understanding of other cultures, the United States, and even yourself. You could choose a program in Africa, Asia, Europe, South America, or some other exotic country on the globe. My study abroad adventure in Seville, Spain was life-changing and the best choice I ever made as a student. A college career just isn't complete without studying abroad.

Studying abroad broadens your perspective beyond the microcosm of college life. And in today's world, you need to see life from a wider view than the piece that you inhabit. Every day the world is becoming smaller because of technological advances. Any international experience is useful whether you use it in your career, or hold on to the experience as a story to share with friends and family. Studying abroad lets you study a foreign language, or learn a new one, from a hands-on perspective and that alone is priceless. If languages aren't high on your priority list, the chance to see a different part of the world and experience a new way of life is equally as valuable.

An added bonus to studying abroad is how the experience will set you apart from the rest of the pack when applying for scholarships, internships and jobs after graduation. Only a small percentage of students study abroad. Be part of that small percentage! Another advantage is that participating in a study abroad program doesn't usually set you back in your academic studies. But even if it does, it is worth the extra semester.

As a student-athlete, the best times to study abroad are during a summer semester or after you've completed your athletic eligibility. However, if you have a good rapport with your coaching staff, it may be possible to study abroad during a regular semester or for a full academic year. Visit your college's study abroad office, research programs on the Web and gather information early into your collegiate career, so you're prepared to discuss your options when you're ready.

From a financial point of view, a study abroad program can be expensive. This shouldn't deter you. There are many ways to reduce, defer or eliminate these costs. Financial aid is an option worth researching. Financial aid includes grants, loans and scholarships. Your university's Financial Aid office can give you more information on available lenders. They can also provide information on grants or scholarships, which are normally distributed by your university, private institutions or private donors. Also inquire with the study abroad office and research at the library or on the Internet. Money is available, but like most things in college, you must proactively seek out what you want. That may also mean finding part-time work or asking for help from your family.

Both internships and studying abroad are life-changing experiences that will transform you into a more confident, well-rounded and cultured person. These are all qualities that will enable your success in college and beyond. So do something out of the ordinary. Explore internships, study abroad, or do both! These experiences will last for a lifetime.

HELPFUL HINTS

1. Begin the internship search and study abroad process early.
2. Obtain multiple internships.
3. Study abroad.

Chapter 9
THE UPS & DOWNS OF BEING A STUDENT-ATHLETE

———

I experienced so many highs and lows as a student-athlete, from the many athletic struggles and frustrations during my freshman year to eventually finding success, that sometimes I wonder how I got through it all. In between, there were many times when I was ready to give in and call it quits, but something inside told me that was the easy way out. I was never an All-American. I'm not a professional athlete today. But these are not indicators of failure. I had many successes on the track in the triple jump and even more success in the classroom. It all translated to the success I enjoy in my career today and it came from persevering, applying myself and never giving in to the pressure.

All of my abilities were used to their full potential. I surprised many who doubted me, but never myself. Deep inside, I knew I could compete at the collegiate level, athletically and academically, and that's exactly what I did. I put a goal in front of me and once I reached it I went to the next one. That's exactly what you must do throughout all of the ups and downs you will face in your career. Keep pushing forward and you'll have no regrets. Never settle for mediocrity and constantly progress toward whatever you're pursuing.

My life as a student-athlete gave me more than I ever imagined. I developed many relationships that will last a lifetime. I created memories I can share with my future children and grandchildren. These are things I will have forever. Believe it or not, the four to five years you spend in college will go by quickly. Don't take it for granted or have regrets when it comes to an end. I took full advantage of everything college had to offer, and although I miss parts of it, the experience is mine, and it can't be taken away. You can have the same thing if you just believe in yourself and never give in. Life is what you make it. Make it wonderful. Be the hammer and not the nail!

HELPFUL HINTS

1. Never give up!

Chapter 10
CONCLUSION

————

It should be obvious at this point that your success as a student-athlete, and in life, hinges on you and your actions. College is a special time in your life. Enjoy your experience to the fullest and take advantage of the many opportunities that come your way. If you apply the advice in this book throughout your college career, or even just a portion of it, you will create positive changes that will benefit you in college and long after it's over. Remember it's important to have an open mind and to remain optimistic. Life is too short to allow pessimism or other people to deter you from your dreams and goals. Be who you are and not something you're not. In the end, you're the one you have to face in the mirror everyday, so be happy and satisfied with what you see! A dream is only as good as your actions to fulfill it.

Always be aware that these years are a period of growth and change. Be prepared for the many crazy twists and turns your life will take. Always remember that during the tough times, there is always support available and during the good times there is always someone to celebrate with. Take advantage of what your university, family, teammates and friends have to offer you: endless support and love.

When you finally get to the top of the mountain and along the way, do your best to help someone else out in their journey to success. Always be willing to lend a helping hand to someone in need, as those who have helped you. Take the initiative to help out the new walk-on or a fellow teammate who is struggling. And don't resist accepting a helping hand, because you'll need it from time to time. Lastly, set an excellent example for upcoming student-athletes who look up to you as a role model. And never forget to thank those who have been instrumental in your success. Without them none of your success would be possible.

College is an experience that you don't want to squander. Make the best of it! You can do that by following these final pieces of advice that summarizes everything I've covered in this book:

1. **Be proactive.** Opportunities won't fall in your lap. You must pursue them.
2. **Be willing.** Open yourself to the many things that college has to offer.
3. **Be resourceful.** It might take a bit of legwork, but you can get everything you need from your college experience.
4. **Be networked.** College is a social experience. Leverage that for enjoyment today and professional success in the future.
5. **Be optimistic.** There will be difficult days, but having a positive attitude will get you through every time.
6. **Be prepared.** Learn how to organize and prioritize your life. It'll pay dividends.
7. **Be a role model.** Set yourself apart from the crowd, and show them how student-athletes get it done!
8. **Be thankful.** You're in a unique position, be grateful for it.
9. **Be persistent.** Never give up, and always progress toward your goals.
10. **Be yourself.** Listen to the advice of others, but realize that in the end, the choice is yours.

Good luck to you and your endeavors, and never give up. You can do it. Have fun!

ACKNOWLEDGEMENTS

Student Athlete 101 would not have been possible without my amazing experience as a student-athlete at Western Michigan University. I would like to thank all of my coaches, teammates, professors and advisors at WMU who inspired me especially Dr. Edward Mayo. This book likewise wouldn't be in your hands without the loving support of my amazing family and friends. Special thanks goes to Laila Al-Arian, Dan Charnas and my editor Michele Dortch. I dedicate this book to all collegiate student-athletes, and wish you success on and off the field.

Antonio Neves - New York City

ABOUT THE AUTHOR

Antonio Neves is an award-winning journalist, producer and writer living in New York City. A graduate of the Columbia University Graduate School of Journalism, Neves has worked for Nickelodeon, NBC, MSN, BET News, Advertising Age and MacNeil/Lehrer Productions. As an undergraduate at Western Michigan University, Neves was an all conference and academic all conference triple jumper.

CPSIA information can be obtained
at www.ICGtesting.com
Printed in the USA
LVHW080519080723
751744LV00003B/636